RICHARD LEWIS

when thought is young

Reflections on Teaching and the Poetry of the Child

19 NEW RIVERS PRESS 92

Edited by C. W. Truesdale
Editorial Assistance by Paul J. Hintz
Cover artwork by Amanda Lewis
Book Design by Gaylord Schanilec
Typesetting by Peregrine Publications

Portions of this book were originally published in *The Minnesota Review*
(Fall, 1971) and in *Parabola* (Vol. IV, No. 3 and Vol. IV, No. 4)

The publication of *When Thought Is Young* has been made possible by
generous grants from the Arts Development Fund of the United Arts Council,
the First Bank System Foundation, Liberty State Bank, the Tennant Company Foundation, and the National Endowment for the Arts (with funds ap-
propriated by the Congress of the United States). New Rivers Press also
wishes to acknowledge the Minnesota Non-Profits Assistance Fund for its
invaluable support.

New Rivers Press books are distributed by:

The Talman Company   Bookslinger
150 Fifth Avenue   2402 University Avenue West
New York, NY 10011   Saint Paul, MN 55114

When Thought Is Young has been manufactured in the United States of
America for New Rivers Press, 420 N. 5th Street/Suite 910, Minneapolis,
MN 55401 in a first edition of 2,500 copies.

To my sister and friend,
Susan West

Introduction

CHILDHOOD is not an easy aspect of growth to define. As adults looking back at childhood, we tend to define its meaning in terms of particular experiences we can remember. At the time I began this book my own children were very young – and I was just starting a career as a teacher interested in reaching the sources of expressiveness and imagination in childhood. In responding to my children's journey through childhood I was always fascinated by the degree to which certain of their actions and thoughts often revealed those basic ideas and impulses that were, in effect, the building blocks of their emerging consciousness. In my own life, I was (and still am) struggling to find a way of bringing into my own consciousness and vocabulary some of the root stirrings of what enables us to be persons of such infinite possibility and expressiveness.

In observing my two children, as well as working with children of all ages in school settings, I was continually confronted with their spontaneous energy, enthusiasm, and playfulness. I was also trying very hard to become aware of what in children causes them to be the children they are – not so much in terms of their individual character, but the elements of their personality, which are somehow the universals of childhood anywhere. What is it in childhood that plants the structures of their later abilities to play, to speak, to imagine, to sing, to dance, to write and to learn? What is this need to express and create things? What in the child is really a desire to reach a consciousness that ultimately brings about an awareness of things and experiences? Not easy questions by any means, but questions that haunted me both as a parent and teacher.

Over the course of a number of years, I tried to gather from notes I took on every day moments, either something my children said or a student wrote, or something as simple as my observing a gesture or situation they evoked in play — and to synthesize these notes into a statement or impression that attempted to find the underlying meaning of what I had observed. While not systematic in any way, these statements soon started an important means of reflection for myself. They often served as a stepping stone into larger and more complicated issues of seeing the child as a learner and imaginer.

In a sense this book is a collection of these reflections arranged to evoke in the reader something of the arc of development that makes up some of the expressive life of early childhood. Not meant to be an academic study, *When Thought Is Young* is my personal odyssey into those elements of childhood that attracted me as the root-stirrings of the interior world of the child.

My decision to make these reflections available in book form comes from the fact that I wanted to share with readers those facets of childhood easily overlooked — and, because of the pressures of our hurried lives, easily forgotten by us. I also wanted, in some modest way, to underscore those aspects of our growing that I believe to be our primary learnings — learnings difficult to locate and to access but that are often the origin of our innate expressive and imaginative abilities.

I have formatted the book so that my own voice is sometimes accompanied by a child's voice. I have included writings by children that have come from my own work with them as well as writings that have been brought to my attention; all in their own way have moved me because of the quality and genuineness of their feelings and thought. The artwork in the book was created by my daughter Amanda when she was between the ages of three and six, and is used now with her gracious permission.

So many persons have contributed to making this book or have helped me shape and support what I am thinking and doing as a writer and teacher. In a sense whether it be the gift of my own children Amanda and Sascha, or the privilege of working with children in schools over these many years, or the fellow teachers and artists I have had the opportunity of collaborating with, or the kindness and encouragement of friends and family — all have been enormously generous in giving of themselves as well as simply being who they are. This book is for all of you — and for those who might find in it some small moment of understanding of what the child — and childhood — can mean to ourselves and to the world at large.

when thought
is young

When you were born, your hands were sea-smelling, your fingers sea-shelled, your palms sea-moist, your cry, crying its sea-birth.

The urgency of what is alive to be in its aliveness, to claim its borning into birth, its birth into becoming. . .

There is in the smell of birth a wetness, a fluid ripeness to ease the birthing, a washing from waters that held it in seed, a damp-ness of earth's moisture. There is in the odor of the born, the blood's flow, bathing birth's wounds. There is in the smell – a wetness, breathing through.

A human is a soul of its own feelings.

— Marina,
Age 9

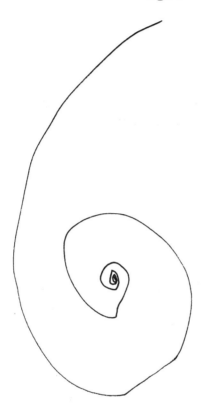

The blur of light
conquers the dark.
I awake dazzled.

— David,
Age 11

. . .the world is a place of new things to do.

— Ellen,
Age 8

As your sensory prowess tries to feel and taste the tentative appearances of light, shadows, smells and sounds around you — you begin to play. . .

*Long, long ago people could
see and feel the stars and sky
because the sky was down so
that people could touch and feel
it.*

— Katherine,
Age 6

The body extends itself through what it touches, explaining the knowledge that is our hand, the awakening that is our touching.

4

Learning as venturing out, hesitating, turning away, venturing in, meeting, grasping, forming. . .

venturing out, hesitating, turning away, venturing in, meeting grasping, forming. . .

As my happiness grows
the sunlight grows also. . .

— Jenny,
Age 9

From your frailty comes the strength of your expressing.

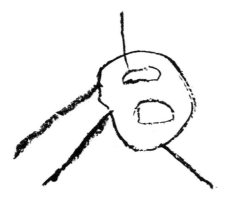

To the child playing alone, silence is a companion, invited to play — so both can share their aloneness.

From our aloneness, our desire: desiring to speak so that we may hear our selves speaking – our speaking, desiring to be heard by our silence.

A child is the privacy of a universe learning to talk to itself.

In his room, in half darkness, he gropes with sounds. Standing in his crib, he and the receding light converse. Speckles of sound – shadows quickly swirl across the room, missiles of whispers dart and disappear, laughter and crying pinch into suddenness. Sounds bend, and break open, sounds reach to melody and fade to murmurs. His thirst for pause. The light is gone. He sleeps.

Our expressiveness implies expression not yet expressed — wordless possibilities still to be brought to conception, let alone birth.

Time is nature, forming itself in calendars of its own devising, proposing necessity, inventing those spaces for something. . .to begin.

Sound as image, no more and no less than itself. The child playing with sounds, tripping them from her tongue till they fluster next to her, congregating into a mixture of moving air, about to become, something more. . .

From what conversation without words does language come? From what recess of depthful thought and feeling does it find its way to consciousness? From what intuition does it pressure itself through intimation into appearance, bringing itself upward into that small spring from which the drinker not only drinks — but which, in clear light, he begins to see himself?

Glimpses of felt-shadows through which we move, with only a memory of a shadow to guide us to what we want to know, what we want to say.

The day you heard the sound of your own voice talking — startling you into hearing your own speaking. . .talking for you.

Does a child see the distance between herself and her words — the amount she must travel before she reaches the words that are her own? Does she sense that language is something that must be reached for, and, just when she thinks she has found it, it escapes her, waiting in hiding so that she can reach for it again?

How varied must be the conversations of the world: the talking between people, the playing of talk, talking coming from someone, tones and rhythms of people talking, silences in talking, hands and faces moving in talking, words inside talking, someone listening and someone talking, all of it happening again and again. And those other conversations: wind and trees, clouds and sky, fish and water, moon and night, earth and leaves, talk of one thing to another, events into events, reactions into reactions, meanings into meanings. And somewhere in this intricate web of voicings, the child begins to take part in the making and receiving, in the turning of thoughts, in the fashioning of response. He becomes the converser conversing, talking with himself, through himself, out of himself, finding, finally, partners for the onrush of his talking.

As it leaves her mouth at last to become real, a "word" to a child must be the final accumulation of hundreds of silent discoveries – compact and crystalline in its appearance, light and easy to hold, delightful in its taste and fragrance.

In the space of a word is its weight – its breath of meaning, breathing through us, weightlessly changing the spaces of our silence.

Space dares the child to enter it — and the child discovering his limbs, makes them into the vocabulary of his body, able to challenge the daring of space.

Children are their bodies, filled with the feeling of their bodies. Children are their bodies in the orbit of their eventual bodies. . .

In your crawling you think that you can do better — crawling until you happen upon the accident of doing better, learning that the accident can be the startling event that makes you stand up. . .

The earth turns around
Like a ripple
And swings
Through moon-space.

– Bruce,
Age 8

Playing is the most precise moment of what is important about now.

To play is to experience process shedding its own skin.

A child plays in silence, while silence plays around the child. Together they make a conversation.

How infinite and minutely constructed are the impulses which pull us from our silence to our speech, from our stillness to our moving, from our grasping to our playing.

Play needs no justification, no moral rationale that it is good to have around because children might, in their enjoyment of play, be learning something useful. Play has its own reasons for existence. It manifests its qualities not because we have ordained it with purpose, but because it comes of its own accord and with its own instinctual reasoning, at the childhood of human growth.

To the child her play is her poetry — a poetry not concerned with the exactness of language but with images being lived in and made alive, a poetry not of subtle combinations of sounds but of voices imitating and seeking other voices, a poetry not of the working out of metaphor but of a state of being which is a metaphor, a poetry not of contemplation but of drama unfolding, a poetry not only of the ordering of experience but of experience ordering itself — a poetry, made constantly, used now, finished and begun again, a poetry always changing because it, and what in the child has to grow and change, are of one and the same source.

Whenever my two-year-old daughter saw a bird or a dog, anything that had an eye, she would stop, and moving her hand to her eye would say one of her first words – "eye." The saying was as much in the vocalization of the word as in her hand's gesture: word and gesture inseparable.

The child names, enclosing itself inside the named, known by what it has named, as namer.

What links us together, as well as defining our separateness, is our speaking between us.

Sound does. It is a doing. A vibration of air doing and done. Sound is made by a doing. A coupling of stillness and movement. Sound does what it can. A coming and going. Sound reaches. It startles silence. Sound shapes itself. Its shaping, another doing. My son, watching us talking, asks his first question: "Doing?"

Each question becomes its own teacher.

Your walking takes you, takes you to your belonging more to your coming and going, to the steady balance of your footsteps traveling with your body, learning to walk to your own time, in step with your own space.

As my son scribbles, his breathing quickens. He is the axis upon which all of the world's motion is focused and through him moving.

Scribbling, his lines like tendrils uncoil from in themselves to their searching. . .outside.

Children create to express their manifold excitement with creation.

I made a tree with
a lot of colors.
It is just beginning.
It is very small.

– Pablo,
Age 7

The child is his own inspiration, inspired by what he touches,
touching what in himself, inspires.

Children feel into their life. Textures of thought, feeling their way into being expressed.

Content with her afternoon nap still draped around her shoulders, my daughter announces: "I had a dream that I was a spiral — and everyone drawed me."

To learn is to express, learning is the expression of learning, to learn is to extend, extending is expressive of our reaching, expressiveness is our reaching to our learning. Learning and expressiveness cause each other.

They dance and sing a continual geometry — shapes and forms from which their thoughts tenaciously cling — galaxies spinning exuberance.

Do children sing to give sound melody or do they want melody because in everything there is melody — enticing them to take it and sing it back into sound?

Our son thinks the piano "sings" a "song" — with words being the gestures of a giraffe, a clown or a monster dancing. The enchantment of music becoming the thing it expresses — music becoming a song whose lyrics are no more than gestures made into a dance of what they, as gestures, intend to become. . .as words.

There is a music in play, an intimate unwinding of themes and melodies, a counterpoint between persons and objects, a rhythm which shifts and sways to an unexplained forward motion. Children move into this music as if it were one long continuous phrase existing always with or without them — a fusion of dissonances and consonances in which their playing, relentless in its improvisations, is always intent on creating even more original harmonies than those already heard.

To improvise is to have faith in what exists, allowing possibility to glean the best of itself.

As your body is now more than itself, it exerts itself in larger motions, so that your running stretches into your vigor, shouting speedily through your body.

I hear our children wrestling, their bodies tumbling out through yells and cries on to an open field receiving them in the green sweat of its body, desiring towards summer.

From their alertness in being, their intensity of exuberance, their sensual awareness – from this animality do children root their humanness.

They're running in circles. In circles, ever widening circles, like sound having to push outwards. They're pursuing themselves by pressing away from themselves. The circular motion, the comfortableness of going around and around. They're discovering the circle in which all ends meet. Ends meeting, but in the middle, a center on which the circle rests. Ends no longer ends but beginnings of a whole — no longer beginnings but what is continuous. Children running through wholeness, feeling its familiarity, as if it were nothing but themselves. Children running in circles, keeping time to their ancient rite of making the universe their own.

Children recognize the wild because they are of wildness, played into dreams, imagined into speaking, thought into memory.

Play is passion given order, played out passionately.

Our roots are our human past deepening in search of our living past — our living past that is the seed from which life — first found itself alive.

I found a puddle and made it into a pond and I put an island in it.

— Sean,
Age 7

Children inhabit the day, as they do the moment, inhabiting the whole of its house — and there to be lived in.

Play is the pursuit of depth to its depthfulness — a channeling of vision into insight, a concentration of experience into experiencing.

The graveling of children in mud. Their desire to be muddy, to be fully in the mud, mud-coated and mud-soaked. Their seeking the sensations of mud being squished, stepped on, stepped in, of sinking and rising, the slushing of sucking sounds. Their penetrating the sloppiness of the earth, the ooze of creation, the appearance of shapes. This watery dirt holding itself onto their smooth skin, making it blotched with strangely moving fissures of dark liquid flows. Rubbery and malleable, the mud is their island about to be formed, turned and folded into mud kingdoms flushed out by hands and feet digging furiously in muddiness — before the coming of sunlight and heat bake it all into a solid crust — caked and dried into a home for hundreds of hungry ants.

In this creatured world there are children discovering what it must be like to be the ant crawling into its hideaway, while also sensing their difference from the ant, as they, themselves, hide — clustered inside their curiosity, watching and talking about the ant. . .crawling.

A little tree was hidden behind leaves. When the worker came to rake the leaves the tree flew away. It landed in an anthole. The ants came over where the little tree was. The ants climbed where the little tree was. The tree made friends with the ants.

— Chris,
Age 8

26

The sky is anxious with vibrancy, restless in its stillness, massing toward change. The child, looking up, finds herself in a sky of her own solitude.

The snow is
God's pillow breaking
like shooting stars
going backwards.

— Sascha,
Age 7

The need for children to become aware of their insights into change — daylight getting lighter, age getting older, wind shifting, water drying, clouds evolving — and from these insights the knowledge that these perceptions can give meaning to their sensibilities.

At approximately the same age, around a year old, both of my children during the summer spent a great deal of time at a stream picking up small stones – and carrying them a few feet away. There was such concentration in their picking up each stone and then throwing or placing it somewhere else, that I could sense, aside from the physical pleasure of being able to hold those jagged and rounded weights, a serenity in their now being able to change the order of the stones into new order. Perhaps, playing with those stones was their first intimation of all things in nature acting upon some other thing. Becoming part of that process, they had become alive to another prospect of their creating.

When children play they make a virtue of simplicity as they create play from what is at hand – admitting by playing that there is always something there, ready to be gathered by their playfulness into something that can be played with.

The child prepares his world by mixing it into miniatures. He tastes it in small proportions, seeing what flavors can be found in its smallest places. He digests the smallness, letting himself be absorbed within it, moving as it moves, through the stomach of larger bodies, passing into the linings of vessels connecting to other bodies, nourished continually by these entities of smallness, each contained as a world, tasted.

....*stones in water*

The simplest point of attraction, a speck of dust, a shadow, a hand, a single thread, a ring – these can become for children beginnings of immense proportions. They see them as having a history, a past, a nature peculiar to themselves as "things." They care about their origins, their "whyness," the "how" of their creation. The child's seriousness about these things takes us in and past dreams, routing us into thinking that moves with intuition, with images revolving in a free-floating world, with feeling extending itself often to perceptions formed in a time far from our own. And the further the child gets into these things, the greater her excitement, as if she senses the extent of her wisdom, the meaning of her knowledge, the closeness with which she, without warning to any of us, quietly finds who and what she is – revealing that special relationship between herself and the things of the world that is the secret of her being.

As poet and scientist the child investigates what is inside of all that is outside in order to touch the inward of all that is outward, finding his way into and out of what is continually, touching us.

In an attempt to relieve the energy that she has discovered, that she is a discoverer who has discovered the excitement of uncovering and happening upon a phenomenon, an idea, a feeling, an event, a circumstance – that could not and would not exist without her act of discovering, the child, conscious of her power to discover, finds that her only relief, is more discovery.

I Like Nature

Flowers come with nature.
Trees come with nature.
We come with nature.

– Donna,
Age 7

The generosity of the child in his shuffling particulars and specifics with his hands, in his arranging and clarifying with his eyes and ears. The delicacy of the child in his adding of differences, subtracting of quantities, equaling of sames, dividing of wholes. The pleasure of the child to sort and filter, to design and devise elements from elements, breaking them down and building them up to their sums and totals, complicating and simplifying them to their proportions and dimensions, taking and giving to the world, its parts and pieces, assembled slowly and carefully by each child, thinking and feeling towards his equations of reality.

This new flower, fondled by discovery, held close to the eye's touching, felt by tips of smell, heard by finger's playing, the making of it known, the known of it understood, the known of it becoming, this flower. . .as everything else, new and as never before, waits its turn, ready to be found, in its newness, by this child.

Sprouting at the earth's crust a flower became what it intended to become — following what in itself was, flowering.

Having assigned his body to the flower's body, our son asks:
"Where is the flower's mouth?"

The flower is a petal seeking heat seeking
water greedy plant known as a FLOWER.

— Anon.

What the Flower Smells Like

It smells new and watery like a pond. It smells quiet
and whistles and snaps in cold or wind. It smells
comforting.

— Caroline,
Age 8

I didn't know there was another me in the world. It
seems like every time I smell a flower I see myself.

— Jill
Age 10

Slowly, as she dances, she bends from inside something of a tree. Turning upon turning, she brings from her growing the weight of her limbs, stretching to her singing, something of a tree and something not a tree, something else, as she dances, that is hers alone — and alone she found, when it fell from the tree.

A bird's shadow goes into the shadow of an oak.
The tree has a new twig.

— Jimmy,
Age 10

The poetic moment as translucent — wordless yet explicit in meaning, a moment in which the reasoning of another logic proves through sensation — yet another idea of existence.

Early one morning when the birds were singing
I had another heart in me.

— Anon.,
Age 8

What children create is from the "doings" of childhood — it is a doing of consciousness, of consciousness making itself, of consciousness displaying its appearance, of consciousness becoming conscious. What children create is in the natural order of creation, and the materials of their creation cannot be separated from the creation of themselves. They "make" things because without making there is no feeling of the self making itself, no feeling of things in relation to other things, no feeling of changing and transforming something in order to reach its particular "self," no feeling of the engagement in the process which is themselves, affecting and recreating from themselves, the furthering of the human — in themselves.

Mmm. . . . it's marvelous!
It's magical!
With my paintbrush
I unfold the sky,
I unfold the earth.
I make the sun shine;
I make the river flow.

— Anon.,
Age 7

Art is magic. Suddenly you say, you think, "I want to do something. What is the best thing to do? Art, will it do this, will it do that — and that's art."

— Alex,
Age 6

As my daughter lets the lines of her drawing extend and twist their way into circles, out of and into which two eyes blink, a mouth opens, two hands stretch, two feet stand, and the sky and the sun and the moon meet, she quietly whispers, "My pencil is growing."

To the child the power of the poetic, the power of the mythic, is a deeply physical presence entering through her and around her. The child does not simply imagine these powers, she becomes the powers themselves, asking them to be the source of her whole being.

For a child to want to become a butterfly while dancing is not simply a fantasy of childhood. It is childhood finding what part of the butterfly still remains dancing in childhood.

I saw a beautiful
butterfly that flow
and blow through the
purple sky, and
glided so wide that
the air
not dare to blow.

— Adam,
Age 7

What we notice, we notice not because we were asked to, but because it was there in front of us — and it became apparent that it had more to do with us than anything that was specifically brought to our attention.

Watching the watchful eyes of a frog, these children are brought inside a community of their own curiosity.

Our imagining is surely a physical act. We can no longer think of the imagination as something peculiarly "mind," enclosed within the confines of mental activity. Imagining is the possibility which turns my whole body around from where it might be standing, transforms it to some "otherness," and causes the rhythms of my breathing to change as I fulfill the extent of what I imagine.

I am telling our children a story before they go to bed. Sitting in front of me, they listen.

" . . .and the bumble bee went down the tunnel in the middle of the yellow of the egg. . . "

They listen and their eyes watch me.

" . . .and down in the tunnel in the middle of the yellow of the egg was a stairs. . . "

They listen and their eyes move with me.

" . . .and at the bottom of the stairs was a small door. . . "

They listen and their eyes are waiting.

" . . .and the bumble bee saw a small crack of light underneath the door. . . "

They listen and their eyes are searching.

" . . .and slowly the bumble bee bent down to look through the crack. . . "

They listen and their eyes are a question.

" . . .and do you know what he saw?"

"What?" they whisper, their eyes and my eyes held together by an answer just a step of silence from them.

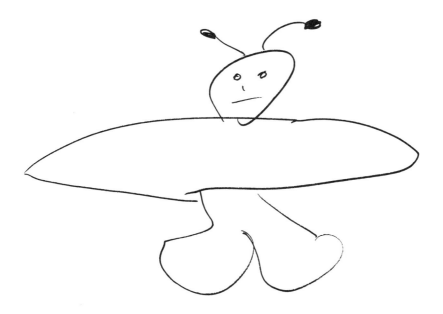

With the grass nearly as tall as you, you wove yourself inside it. Unafraid of these green stalks surrounding you, you turned green corners, coming upon deeper green. Your small hands parted the greenness, pulling it with you as you lay down. And when you sat up, the grass sat up with you. And when you looked at the grass, the grass looked at you. Wavering between green and greenness, you stared at the grass, for there you were – aware only of this.

Children invite mystery, they invite opportunities for the incongruous, the unexplained, the half-revealed, the not knowing, the impending moment, the fear of the hidden, the tension of waiting, the anticipation of surprise, the possibility of danger, the savoring of darkness, the games of guessing, the condition of secrecy. And like explorers on a perilous cliff they lean over its edge looking for what will appear, hanging to every surge of suspense, frozen in their gaze, as the unexpected slowly takes their breath away.

As the moon sometimes does — the question of why — meditates us.

We are encircled by what remains invisible, clothing our nakedness.

We are vulnerable to the whims of the unknown striking us.

You, in your shell of white sheets, cry at how your dreams spread their voices across your sleep, waking you, afraid.

Between the known and the unknown is that tension upon which pivots our desire to express, that balance upon which emerges the meaning of our expressiveness.

Our relationship to the world is our imagining — the world, imagined into existence.

From out of the womb's nightful time, the child brings with him something of his original darkness. Even after birth, the darkness does not recede, but becomes part of the child as he gropes with what makes him afraid of what he imagines of the dark. Picking his way through night's shadows and night's voices, he creates the imaginary, that vision which is his guide into the unknown, making it into what is known and able to be seen by the light of his imagining.

Subject of Thought

If you get into a small boat, from almost anywhere,
you must try your hardest to find some water. After you
have done this you must take off down a channel of thought.
You may make it whatever you suggest. As you begin to
move much faster you forget completely about the boat,
until it's not there. The wind breathes hard now and you
can see something distant in the beyond.

Now you have reached the shores of your mind, and
the sands of the beach are white.

The coral reefs to each side of your head are covered
with many dreams. (You make of these as you wish.) The path
before you is of a sharp incline, but you feel as though
it could be steeper, the pathway is tiring.

After sleeping for a good time, you walk down the path
to the coral, pick a dream, go back to the boat, and
— sleep more, as you float down the channel homeward.

— John,
Age 10

The secret of my imagination is that the things
of the universe are the things of you.

— Charles,
Age 6

43

Often the first thing our children told us in the morning were their dreams, as if their dreams had been suspended lengthwise from the night to the day — and holding on to them, they climbed, one word after another, back into the morning — at last, safely arrived in. . .

In her daydreaming, she talks to herself. Between who she is, and who she isn't, she hears the words she speaks spoken to who she might be. Listener and speaker, she is all in one, crouched in the secrecy of her dream.

Then without warning, she stops. She drinks her juice, asks what we are going to do today, bites into her toast, scoops the egg from its shell, leaves the table and goes into another room.

The day was startled to continue. . .

Our son dances — stomping the ground in order to penetrate the rhythms he's making, stomping as if to listen to the shadows of the earth's heartbeat. . .

Children bring with them the most archaic of histories, intuited mythologies of the earth attempting to expand, waters about to be stirred, air starting outward. . .

To Be Alive

It was there
Something — happened
What was it
A bird
A fish
A lizard
Was it the girl
Listen.
I hear it again
It is the wind
Wind.
It created me
I am its friend
The wind lives
in a secret garden
far away from me
It comes and I sleep
Sleep and the wind and I
drift to air.

– David,
Age 10

To be born is to feel like a seed of corn planted for the first time.

— David,
Age 9

The child reaches back, asking where she was born, how did it feel, where did she come from, how did she get there, what was there before, what was inside, was it dark there, how did it happen. The child reaches back as if to tell herself that she really began, that she was beginning somewhere, that her growing has begun, that she is, because she began.

To be born is happiest in a place full of angels. To start a new life. To remember what may come

— Tony,
Age 9

It is the child who has brought with him and keeps in himself the last of a message he overheard in the confusion of voices before he was born.

When I was a tree in the dark forest,
I saw the beginning of the world.
Then some leaves fell on the ground,
And I saw the beginning of the end
of the world.

— Anon.,
Age 9

Who knows where monsters were born — perhaps in the screaming cyclone of energy that may have been the earth's own birth.

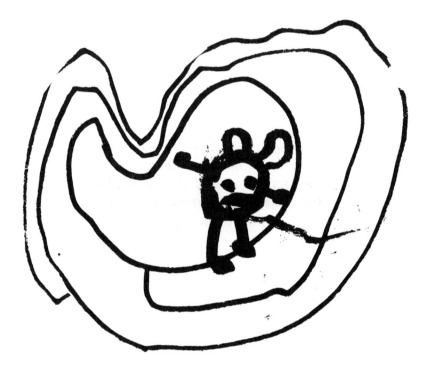

By making the terrible terrifying, children turn their innocence into the serious able to laugh.

The child's way of transposing belief into believing is to "make-believe," pursuing all the alternatives of belief in order to make a choice for believing.

It was hard to really see and feel the real way
you used to live because you live differently now.
If you were part of your old life you would see it
more clearly and you would understand it more.
Also you would feel that you belong, but now
you don't because you belong to your new life.
You are going further on, leaving your old life
behind. It is like looking back on your life.
I saw big clouds of darkness. There was a hole
in the darkness. It got bigger and bigger.
Sometimes I saw dinosaurs who still lived there.

– Allison,
Age 10

The first dot was the dinosaurs
and the world
went around
older
until
there were houses
and people
all over
the world.

– Anon.,
Age 7

Holding their rubber toy animals, they are sprawled on the floor playing as ferocious lions, tigers, elephants and monkeys who chase and hide, growl and purr, leap and jump, attack and retreat, each struggling and fighting to be the most powerful and fearsome of all the animals — animals whose rubber toy faces are masks for what these children so easily and desperately, so instantly and accurately. . .disclose.

Becoming her images the child learns how to stand at a distance from them, feeling in that place and time, the separateness of her becoming, herself.

As they run — they dart, they circle, they crisscross, becoming in an instant. . .flying birds. In some of their faces, the ecstasy of commanding the sky makes them smile — while others race with the look of creatures about to lift-off into flight. Occasionally one of the birds falls to the ground, stunned by the insult of motion to interrupt itself, and then, just as he is about to whimper and call out for help, a whirlwind of wings flying overhead draws him once again upward into the sky. Could they go on like this forever? Will they fly themselves breathless? Shortly, one of the flock veers off from the others, slowing down just enough to cry, "I wanta be a lion now."

There is a craving in children to receive images – to take from the world its many and varied pictures of itself. But just as they are willing accepters, so too do they crave to give, to project onto the world their images, to bring those pictures of their minds to the companionship of someone who can receive and is able to acknowledge their gift of images, who can help at the birth of that trust which enables the imagining self to communicate because it knows that it belongs in the world and to the world, making and taking of the world, its fullness.

To the child, the future must loom in front of her as a light seeping under a closed door – a strangely inviting mystery she is continually in awe of.

Drawing a picture this child draws time to himself, forming it into an image as a portion of time which has become his... withheld, momentarily, from timelessness.

Children can turn anything into anything. For this gift we call them magical, born alchemists of the spirit. But they are more than this: they are the first real inventors – and each child in her own time invents the world all over again, as if it had never been made before.

51

"Look at this writer thing," my son says to me, picking up a stick, and scratching in the dirt, diagonal lines joining.

"What is this?" he asks.

"It looks like an *H*," I tell him.

As we continue my answers to him are about *S*s and *P*s and *O*s.

After awhile I walk on and looking behind me I see him, still turning the ground into a quilt of letters and numbers, spelling and figuring proportions and shapes, making the earth a place to be written on, decorated humbly and boldly, by his hands first learning to write on the surface of its history.

The clouds float towards me
The flowers raise their heads
It rains
And the root fingers are waiting.

— Anon.,
Age 5

Children leap from expression to expressiveness when the very limitations of what they can express are surmounted by what they want to express – so that the content of their expression, in that moment, determines the shape of their expression – in no other possible way than in the instant it was expressed.

The rain is like dragonflies flying backwards down. Stripes of them.

– Anon.,
Age 6

In all expression the argument of what can be expressed, fighting to the last, in what is expressed, struggling as expression, to be understood.

The contented innocence of children has been greatly exaggerated: there seems to be in the pull and tension of their everyday living a suffering, a rising and falling from high exaltation to deep grief that in its sheer energy would be difficult for most adults to sustain in the brief time it takes a child to move from one extreme to the other.

Given a secretive sense, children need to retire into secret, to corner their selves, to hide in their selves, to feel nestled in their privacy. They need an image of themselves confined in themselves, only seen and found by themselves. They need a secreted place to huddle close to their secret dreaming...of dreams dreamt only by themselves, dreaming.

As these children play their games of being dead and alive, our life and death is performed as rituals given ceremony and celebration, ordained with time and space — acquiring, through playing, the outer and inner dimensions of our lives.

Life

Life is a world of
dying and living, which sings
as it runs to die.

— Barbara,
Age 10

Death

Death is like complete blackness. It is light
and then nothing but blackness. It's like sudden
nothingness. It's fast nothingness.

— Alex,
Age 8

A day is when my eyes go back to me.

— Matt,
Age 7

Everywhere I look
I see things
And even when
I close my eyes
I still see things.

— David,
Age 5

Questions arise from the sense of what questions might answer
— the feeling that beyond what is immediately perceived is yet
another perception, perceivable.

He did not understand me when I said the word "invisible." I
took him aside and asked him to blow some air on his hand.
He smiled. He had felt the invisible, without ever having any
need to see it.

Our son begins to cry uncontrollably as we walk along the beach,
for fear that the ocean, like some swollen eye, will blink him
away from us. I try to calm him down by singing a song to him:

> "Water, water, water
> blue, gray and white water,
> water, water, water. . ."

His crying stops. He turns his head cautiously — and for the first
time looks straight ahead at the ocean — singing our words faintly
back to the sea.

Hovering with uncertainty, children ask of meaning, "why?" — only to discover in meaning yet another question, hovering with uncertainty, yet to be asked.

Before there was thunder and lightning, there was just darkness — it was nothing to see and nothing you could ever see, and it would make you feel all alone. The darkness is a mystery that can't be solved.

> — Alicia,
> Age 11

The width and depth of the subjective cannot be measured, being that space in which we are, filling our presence more than we could ever fill it.

The star belongs to the sky,
The sky to the angel,
The angel to my heart,
My heart to myself,
Myself to poetry,
Poetry to something unknown.

> — Anon.,
> Age 11

Once feeling is neglected, learning cannot become process, thought cannot become knowledge. Our humanness exists in the recognition of feeling – and to live otherwise is to debase and deny our struggle to be human.

There is an emotion, the base of all other emotions, it is an emotion of quietness, without thought or sound, disturbed only by another emotion.

– Rick,
Age 10

There must be a time for stillness in our learning – a retreating in order to listen to the stillness in ourselves, hearing our own presence, as it finds its way through the stillness of its searching.

The Old Rock

*I think that if you went deep into the rock, not cutting
it, but just going into it, you would come to a place where time
and things are as one. Because the very deepest deepness of it
is as old as young — which is very young. Young is, well, older
than this world — by far, it is older than time itself.*

*Maybe once, long, long, long ago, when Thought was young —
(and Thought is one of the oldest things there is, far older than
time, time is as new as a flower coming up compared to thought.)*

*The rock was big, bigger than the center, because it was bigger
than everything, and the center is part of everything. Then,
second after second, year after year, age after age, the rock
got smaller, parts of it didn't break off — No! Nothing like
that, it just sort of went inside itself, even as a person sometimes
goes inside itself. So really, the smaller it gets,
the wiser it gets, full of past wisdom and other stuff.*

— Jessica,
Age 10

We are of a childhood still growing, still beginning what in us, still moves towards beginning.

The rain is making a new world

— Patricia,
Age 6

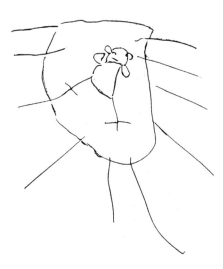

Light vanishes, its last shadows tiring themselves upon us. Our child, pushing back sleep, sings us through the dark, singing over and over again:

In my life
I love my life
My life and you
You and me

61

Afterword

IN THE EARLY fall of 1990 I, along with members of the teaching staff of The Touchstone Center, had the opportunity of working with a group of children at a public elementary school in New York City. Located on the Lower Eastside of New York City, in an area well known for its infestation of crime and drugs, the school serviced a large number of 'homeless' children – as well as children who had been unduly battered by many of the cruelties of inadequate care and support offered to the poor. Our task was to use the arts as a way of bringing these children closer to their innate desire to read and write. Our hope was to also activate their desire to be themselves as children – to learn, if one can call it that, to play and imagine again. What we were not prepared for, as we worked with these children, was not only how much they wanted the resources we were bringing them, but also how necessary this was to their personal survival. Week after week, in classroom after classroom, our presence was anticipated with enormous enthusiasm. (Teachers told us of instances where some children would come to school only on the days we were there.) We were consistently moved by these children's extraordinary concentration and involvement whether it was when they were drawing their imagined magic flower, or making up a story about a creature who lived in the East River. In so many instances, those children considered by their teachers to be uncooperative, inarticulate and uncommunicative became the very opposite.

I should not have been surprised – having seen this kind of thing happen many times before when the arts were offered as that unique and special language of ourselves. But, like all of us, I needed to be reminded of the power these activities have when they are part of an individual's discovery of a personal way of perceiving. It will not be easy to forget the faces of many of these children who, when having said something they had not thought about or said before, became totally transfixed and relaxed with genuine pleasure and satisfaction.

I mention all of this because it was at this time that I began working once again on the present book — a project I had completed, in large part, some fifteen years earlier. My interest in reapproaching this book was based on a strong feeling that much of what I had tried to speak about and define then, both as a parent and teacher of poetry and the arts in general — was in the 1990s becoming increasingly important to those of us who continue to work with children as teachers and artists in the educational realm. Despite the enormous strides in bringing the arts to children in the late sixties and seventies and part of the eighties — and focusing our attention on the child and the child's needs — I feel we are drifting back to a way of thinking that emphasizes various systems of accountability over the innate meaning of the creative process for the child. We are increasingly preoccupied with having to justify the expression of the child's imagination within the context of what we mean by serious learning so that I have been questioned by adults and occasionally challenged by children as to the future usefulness and practicality of "imagination" in their own and children's lives.

Some of what is happening in our attitude towards childhood is due, I believe, to the dramatic evolution of society in our lifetime. There is no doubt that the speed and clarity of electronic communication has depersonalized much of what used to be communicated more slowly and intimately between individuals. The 'entertainment' quality of the media has drawn children, like moths to light, into a passivity where the world often floats by in a train of abrupt images rarely reflected upon by the individual child. As we become more sophisticated in our ability to create technology, we change the way a child experiences and ultimately makes sense of that experience. We are, often without realizing it, distancing children from their own innate skills of play and invention, and their ability to use their senses and their imagination as a form of knowing and understanding. We have begun to use our educational institutions as ropes a child must climb in order to succeed in the competitive marketplace – rather than a place and experience to help children come to a broader view of each other and themselves, and the lifelong creative, learning, and imaginative abilities inherent in all human beings.

And so when this book was begun almost two decades ago, it was not conceived as an educational or pedagogical statement but as personal reflection on the child's growing expressiveness and consciousness. I was, at that time, teaching drama and writing at an independent and racially integrated elementary school in New York, as well as working on various book projects. I had already published *Miracles* and *Journeys* (collections of poetry and prose by children of the English-speaking world) and many of the books I was then editing were based on my interest in making accessible the poetry and poetic traditions of cultures other than our own. I was also involved in teacher training, particularly as it related to helping teachers think and act upon the nature of their own imaginations and the children they teach.

While preparing this present edition, I came across a draft I had made of a possible introduction, that, in rereading it now, helps in locating the impetus behind my composing *When Thought Is Young*. I see how much I wanted to pursue a line of thinking that seemed crucial to me and the future direction my work was eventually to take – and how these same thoughts and questions are still pertinent to me as a foundation to the teaching and writing I am presently pursuing:

When I taught drama and writing at an independent school in New York, I held my classes two or three days a week in a large room with large windows, a piano, some wooden benches and a few folding chairs that went along with two folding tables. The children came to me, at first, grade by grade on a mandatory basis, and then voluntarily. I initially worked with the children in a somewhat formal way, planning ahead of time what I would do with each group. I soon discovered that the children were asking a different role of me — they did not want me to teach poetry and drama but for me to be an active listener to what they wanted to say. They would often come into the room with a variety of feelings that would have little to do with what I had planned for that day — and sometimes the conflict would become so severe that much of the time was spent just trying to come to some working relationship. Of course I was troubled by this conflict — not knowing what it was that I was supposed to be doing with these children and worried that I was not serving either the children or the school very well.

One day a group of very angry eight-year-old children came into the room. Some of them were sulky, some were very verbal and abusive to each other, some went off into corners by themselves. Their anger was uppermost with them, and no pleading on my part could convince them that my wish to teach them writing and drama would make them feel any better. I had no choice but to talk with them about their anger — and talk they did, for they were full of an incident, about how their teacher had disciplined them for misbehaving. This had angered them deeply.

It was while they were talking that I became aware of what they were actually syaing; their words were fully expressive and

accompanied by impassioned gestures and bodily movements tell-
ing me the extent of what they felt. ("She's not going to tell me
what to do", "It's not fair, we were just kiddin' around", "I'm never
coming back here no more".) I listened and then suggested that
maybe they would like to recreate the incident in question. I saw
something I hadn't seen before: they put together their drama with
a minimum of effort, assigning parts and actions with an extraor-
dinary amount of cooperation and sense of purpose. Tables were
moved, chairs set up, lights flicked off, curtains drawn, people
assigned spaces — all with the efficiency of a group that knew where
it was going and what it wanted to do. And then the whole drama
of the incident was acted out improvisationally, each of the children
knowing instinctively when to come in, when to exit, what to say,
what intonations and nuances to create. Children, who during
the year had been too shy to participate or unwilling to be a part
of the group, suddenly were part of what was happening, excelling
in ways I had never seen before. I was asked to accompany the
drama on the piano — improvising along with them musical
characterizations that served as a bridge from one incident in their
drama to another. We were, in one burst of energy, in this together,
and as I followed them in what unfolded I became aware of how
they were moving each other into what each individual had felt
when they first came into the room. They took the greatest care
to respect each other — to keep their play the focus for what they
wanted to express. At the end of the hour, the door opened and
the next group of children was ready to come in — and when they
did, without saying anything they sat down, as an audience
— and they too were caught in the power of what was being por-
trayed. They listened, as only children can listen to each other
when they are speaking through a language that defines and ex-
presses themselves.

*A number of similar situations occurred during the year —
and I realized that as a teacher and learner I had to understand
more completely the role I played and could play with these
children. I began to feel that we could not dictate how a child should
express itself but that a child's expressiveness had to come from
the child — and the very nature of the expressiveness went much
beyond just drama and writing, that it had a crucial connection
to learning and the growing process in each child.*

*I realized how I, in a room by myself with these children, would
have to alter the way I approached them — that somehow I had
to connect to each child, I had to learn how to build from out of
the entirety of the child's ability to communicate and listen more
acutely to those communications that are indeed the child's. I
realized I would have to start at the beginning — at the first tentative grasps of human life toward expression, the first patterning
and shaping of expressiveness, the first elements we, as human
beings, are able to communicate with — and how those elements
might be seen by me in a different light from the way I had been
educated to perceive and use them.*

*I knew that any shift of my perceiving the expressive condi-
tion of childhood would have to evolve slowly through my work
with children — and what indeed I could learn from watching and
participating along with children in their first attempts to
communicate.*

Thinking, once again, about some of the children I am working with now in many of those overcrowded public school class-
rooms — often with little support for the childhood they are so
quickly passing through — I can hear their passionate responses
to our asking them to come back to their "beginnings," to the
point where their language, play, imagining, and creating are
the unquestionable givens of their aliveness. I can also hear

that wonderful chant, when some children had read or performed an original poem or story, or shared a painting or a puppet they had made, that simple exclamation of affirming what is possible in them — and in us as well — clenching their hands and rising to their feet, saying, "Yes, Yes!"

RICHARD LEWIS

has pursued two major interests: the creating of books and the development of the art of teaching. For both interests, the major impetus has been identifying, encouraging, and sustaining the poetic life of both children and adults. His books, a number of which are classics in their field, range from international collections of original writings by children (*Miracles, Journeys,* and *There Are Two Lives*) to anthologies of poetry of the Inuit (*I Breathe a New Song*) to the poetry of China and Japan (*The Moment of Wonder, Of This World, In a Spring Garden, The Way of Silence,* and *The Luminous Landscape*). Lewis's most recent books include *In the Night, Still Dark: A Retelling of the Hawaiian Creation Myth* and *All of You Was Singing: A Retelling of an Aztec Myth.*

Aside from his books, Mr. Lewis has written articles and essays about the imagination of children, which have appeared in *Childhood Education, Young Children, Elementary English, Connecticut Scholar, Minnesota Review, National Education Association Journal, Orion Nature Quarterly, Parabola, Parnassus Poetry in Review, Psychological Perspectives, Publishers Weekly,* and other journals.

A resident of New York City, Mr. Lewis founded The Touchstone Center for Children in 1969. Deeply committed to nurturing the creative life of each individual, Richard Lewis and The Touchstone Center have pursued a unique approach to curriculum, based on the use of elemental themes as a means of integrating the arts with other disciplines.

Mr. Lewis presents workshops and seminars for adults throughout the United States, and has been on the faculty of the New School for Social Research, Fordham University, Bank Street College of Education, Rutgers University, Western Washington University, Queens College, and Lesley College Graduate School.